# Defense Against
# The Psychopath

*A brief introduction to human predators*

From the book, The Art of Urban Survival

By Stefan H. Verstappen

S. Verstappen

Woodbridge Press

Toronto, Canada

Cover Design: S. Verstappen
All Illustrations by S. Verstappen
Copyright © 2011 by Stefan H. Verstappen
All rights reserved
ISBN 978-0-9869515-2-7

# Surviving Predators

*Life is nothing but a competition to be the criminal rather than the victim.*
Bertrand Russell

In the urban environment, criminals fulfill nature's role of predators. While the strategies criminals use vary widely, there is an important distinction between two types of criminal, the psychopathic, and the non-psychopathic.

The non-psychopathic criminal is the type most familiar to the public. For these criminals, crime is a survival mechanism anthropologists call the *Cheating Strategy*. The Cheating Strategy simply refers to the advantage cheating provides in terms of survival. For example, a person may spend eight hours a day working to earn a certain amount of money, but a thief could spend only a few minutes to gain what another spent eight hours to acquire. The thief's cheating strategy is cost effective – the gains far exceed expenditures.

However, man is a social animal and cheaters are seldom tolerated in a reciprocal society wherein everyone works together for common benefits and equal share in the fruits thereof. Society evolved the institution of revenge and punishment as a counter to the cheating strategy. While some question the effectiveness of punishment as deterrent, on a survival level, punishment factors into the cost/benefit analysis of those considering a cheating strategy. A thief who steals another's wages may be acting cost effectively, but if the thief is subsequently caught and forced to serve five years in prison, he will find the costs now far exceed the benefits.

Therefore, crime prevention requires that we make the costs of using a cheating strategy greater than the benefits by forcing criminals to work harder, and increasing their chances of being caught.

The cheating strategy is often used when people are at a disadvantage. Poverty, low intelligence, and poor education are the root causes of much criminal behavior. Most crime safety and self-defense literature focuses on this type of criminal activity, defense against a mugger, preventing theft, home defense and so forth. This type of crime is logical. One person has something another does not, and so the latter cheats to acquire it. While you cannot condone the methods employed, you can understand the motivation for the actions.

Another type of criminal behavior committed by non-psychopaths are crimes of passion. These acts of violence stem from emotional turmoil and our primitive instincts. Many otherwise average people are capable of committing assault, rape, and murder in the heat of passion especially if fueled by drugs and alcohol. While the acts they commit are pathological, they are not themselves necessarily psychopaths.

However, when it comes to the second type of criminal the underlying motivations become surreal. While psychopaths will certainly use the cheating strategy, it is seldom necessary to their survival. A millionaire psychopath would readily rob a starving child. Obviously, the millionaire's survival is not at stake. There is no obvious logic to what motives could underlie such behavior. Psychopaths often elude justice for this very reason. In criminal trials, the prosecution is required to ascribe a motive to the defendant. However, in the case of psychopaths, their motives are so bizarre and alien that even if a prosecutor could explain it, most jurors would not believe it. The psychopath can also assault, rape, and murder, but it is seldom a crime of passion. It is instead a cold and calculated plan to gain what the psychopath wants.

Of all the criminal types that inhabit our society, the psychopath is by far the most destructive, the most successful, and the least understood. For these reasons, any self-defense program must begin with a study of the most dangerous predator on the planet.

# The Psychopath

*The urge to save humanity is almost always a false-face for the urge to rule it.*

H.L. Mencken

Psychopathy [i] infects the full spectrum of humanity irrespective of race, culture, geography, economic class or personality type. It is distributed in a population in a similar way that left-handedness is. One would not notice a person is left handed until you see him write or catch a ball. Similarly, one may not notice a psychopath until you see him do something that requires them to have a conscience.

Most people think of a psychopath as a rare creature found only in the lowest levels of society. However, the reverse is true. They are not rare, but actually quite common, and you are more likely to find psychopaths in the boardroom than on the wrong side of the tracks. [ii] The reason is that the more competitive a particular environment is, the more ruthless the use of the Cheating Strategy becomes. Within the highest circles of power and wealth, a lack of pity and remorse is practically a prerequisite to success, and only the psychopathic mentality can thrive.

Because of the tremendous destruction psychopaths reap on society, it is vital for everyone to be aware of their existence and to recognize their behavior traits. Understanding them is the first step to defending oneself against them.

**Key Characteristics**

<u>Lack of Empathy:</u> Empathy is the ability to experience within oneself, the feelings and emotions expressed by others. It is what allows us to feel what others are feeling. It is why we are inspired by works of art, music and poetry. Empathy allows us to experience the grandeur of life, to be truly alive, and is one of the defining characteristics of what makes us human.

Psychopaths have no empathy and as a result, they are neither truly human, nor truly alive. When they see 'Normals' admiring a piece of art, or playing with their children, or caring for a pet, or any number of human emotional interactions, they can't understand what all the fuss is about. Psychopaths realize at an early age that they are different, and that they should act as everyone else does in order to be accepted into society. They learn to mimic what they see others do, but they can never understand why they should act this way.

Although they are consummate actors, careful observation will reveal telltale cracks in their façade. They know enough to fake concern when someone is sick, or to pretend happiness when some good fortune befalls a friend, but in situations where the psychopath has no pre-rehearsed act; their adlib often reveals a stunning lack of empathy. For example, if attending a funeral, a psychopath would correctly mimic the same expressions of sadness as the other mourners, but then makes sexual advances towards the grieving widow clueless to the gross inappropriateness of such an action. People with empathy would instinctively understand such behavior as inappropriate. However, the psychopath cannot.

Lack of Remorse: Remorse is an emotional expression of personal regret felt by a person after he or she has committed an act, which they deem to be shameful, hurtful, or violent. This very definition precludes a psychopath from experiencing such a feeling. With no empathy, there can be no emotional expression. Nor can a psychopath feel shame, nor comprehend that anything they do can be hurtful to others.

Psychopaths understand when people are angry with them for their behavior, and as a last resort, they may pretend they are sorry, but unlike most people, they are not the least bit disturbed by feelings of guilt. Remorse is a powerful negative emotion that causes turmoil in those that feel it, turmoil that often results in self-destructive or self-deprecating behaviors. The psychopath may pretend remorse but their real behavior has not changed, they still go shopping, they still go to parties, they have no problems sleeping at night.

Superficiality: Passion drives someone to go further than needed to explore, learn, and master a subject. Most people enjoy listening to music, but it is someone passionate about music that goes on to learn how to play an instrument. Similarly, many people are interested in new technology but only a passionate person goes on to become an engineer. Lacking passion for anything other than themselves, psychopaths can never penetrate beyond the surface of most knowledge. As a result, they exhibit a "superficial" comprehension of some or many subjects but are often seen by true experts as being shallow. This superficiality extends to their attempts at acting normal by exhibiting false emotions through an exaggerated affect.

Grandiosity: Despite being shallow and superficial, psychopaths show no self-esteem issues. Psychopaths live in a falsely constructed worldview in which they are both literally and figuratively god. Often seen as megalomaniacs, they also have an equally overblown sense of entitlement.

Irresponsibility: Psychopaths are irresponsible because nothing is ever their fault. Someone else, or the world at large, is always to blame for all of their problems. This makes sense if you understand that psychopaths think themselves perfect. Nothing wrong can ever originate with them and so logic, the psychopath's logic, dictates that everything bad is always someone else's fault.

Impulsive Behavior: The psychopath's impulsive behavior makes sense in light of their megalomania. In their world, whatever they want now, is good, and whatever they do not want is bad. If a psychopath wants sex and his date will not provide it, then rape is good and the date is bad. If someone has money in his or her pocket, and the psychopath wants it, then robbery is good, and the victim is bad for possessing something the psychopath wanted. If this strikes the reader as insane - it is. One of the earliest writers on the subject of Psychopathy, J. C. Prichard coined the now defunct term, *Moral Insanity* as a way to describe Psychopathy in 1835.

<u>Poor Behavior Control</u>: This characteristic can be misleading since many psychopaths exhibit excellent self control by having to pretend to be 'Normal' for most of their lives. The lack of self-control comes into play when the megalomania causes them to do and behave exactly as they please at any time they have an urge. This brings us to the next characteristic.

<u>Lacking Goals</u>: Another characteristic attributed to the psychopathic personality is the lack of goals, but this can be misleading. Many psychopaths have goals, such as murder two victims at once, sabotage a co-worker, or become president. However, often long-term goals are subverted to short-term goals that are, as described previously, whatever the psychopath wants at that particular moment.

<u>Compulsive Lying</u>: Living at the expense of the rest of humanity would be an impossible situation in a rational society. Psychopaths have solved this dilemma through their premier weapon - lies. Lies hold together their view of themselves, their own private universe, and facilitate their need to live parasitically off the rest of society.

Without empathy, shame, and remorse they are free to lie as often and as outrageously as they please. Normal people would blush, or sweat, or tremble, if they dared stretch the truth to the same degree. However, for the psychopath lying is as easy and natural as breathing. This is why they often pass polygraphs. They do not register the physiological reactions that non-psychopaths would when lying. They are so good at lying they can fool trained psychiatrists and even other psychopaths. What is important to know is that given the right circumstances they can fool anyone.

<u>Manipulative</u>: Hand in hand with the psychopath's extraordinary ability to lie comes the ability to manipulate others for their own benefit. Having spent their lifetime studying us, psychopaths are masters of manipulation and experts on knowing how to push our buttons to use our emotions against us. They use this ability to keep those around them confused, unable to think clearly, and off balance.

Psychopaths also learn very early how their personalities can have traumatizing effects on the personalities of non-psychopaths, and how to take advantage of this for purposes of achieving their goals. Like an electric eel that stuns its prey with an electroshock, psychopath's inhuman personality and uncanny ability to manipulate can psychologically stun their intended victims.

<u>Anti-social Behavior</u>: The very essence of the psychopath is anti-social. Their lack of empathy for other people extends onto society and the environment. Vandalism, pollution, graffiti, animal abuse, environmental destruction, building code violations, reckless driving, and a host of morally and socially unacceptable activities are of no concern to the psychopath.

These then are the basic characteristics that psychopaths exhibit. Bear in mind that few psychopaths will express all of the characteristics, and that non-psychopaths can have many of these characteristics as well.

## Common Types of Psychopaths

While there are as many variations in the personalities of psychopaths as there are among normal people, the following lists some general stereotypes.

Narcissists: The most benign form of psychopathology is pathological narcissism. Narcissists, like the mythological Greek namesake Narcissus, are so overcome with self-love that nothing else in the world matters but them. They need a constant source of *Narcissistic Supply*, which is attention, adoration, recognition, awards, and praise.

There are two basic types of narcissist, the Somatic, and the Cerebral. Somatic Narcissists take pride in their looks and appearance. They will flaunt their sexual exploits, brag of their accomplishments, show off their muscles, and display their toys. They are often health nuts, hypochondriacs and sex addicts. Much of their narcissistic supply comes from having numerous sexual partners, but the act itself, often flamboyant and exaggerated, is nonetheless merely an empty show put on by the narcissist for his or her own amusement. Because of their barren inner life, they continually need new thrills simply for the rush of adrenaline. These thrills range from criminal activity and substance abuse to increasingly bizarre sexual acts.

Cerebral Narcissists love their own minds. They are arrogant, condescending, and 'know-it-alls' that pride themselves on being smarter than everyone else is. Contrary to the somatic type, cerebral narcissists often regard their body and its

11

maintenance as a nuisance and burden and are physically lazy, unfit, and often celibate. Their narcissistic supply comes from fame, notoriety, awards, and displays of wealth to create envy in others.

The danger to the public from narcissists is the drain on energy, time, resources, and emotional wellbeing. A narcissist is interested in a person only for what narcissistic supply that person can provide. They will gladly accept love, attention, affection, adoration, praise, emotional and financial support, but being without empathy, they cannot reciprocate any of it. Any partnership they enter into will always be one sided. Once a person ceases to be a source of narcissistic supply, or a better source comes along, they are discarded without hesitation or consideration. Thus, do narcissists leave behind them a trail of broken hearts, broken dreams, empty wallets, and abandoned children.

The Victim: Commonly used by female psychopaths, (but by no means unheard of among males) is the professional victim stereotype. Preying on what psychopaths see as a weakness in others, sympathy, the female psychopath appears helpless, pitiful, emotionally fragile, persecuted, and sexually vulnerable. She pretends heartfelt gratitude for whatever small kindness strangers provide her, but behind the mask is a cunning, ruthless, and loveless predator. Often using sex as the hook, they can juggle several victims at a time draining them of life and money until there is nothing left, then skipping town to avoid the repercussions.

Con Artists: Not all con artists are psychopaths, but psychopaths make convincing con artists. Being excellent liars, they put that talent to use by cheating others. Without a conscience or remorse to stand in the way, they are free to cheat old women out of their life savings, sell quack cures to terminally ill patients, or shortchange the blind. They are usually charming, articulate and convincing, and make successful salespersons. Unlike the Narcissist, the con artist is not as concerned about love or attention, as money.

There are two types of cons psychopaths engage in the Short Con and the Big Store Con. The Short Con is probably the one that most often comes to mind when thinking about con artists. These are tricks and cheats that require no great intelligence to pull off, such as short changing, bait and switch, and Three Card Monte to name a few.

Psychopaths that have a higher intelligence level and/or come from a more respectable background are more likely to establish the Big Store Con. These are large-scale frauds that all rely on a basic strategy. Take something of little to no value, artificially inflate the perceived value, sell to gullible investors, take the money and run. Traditional big store cons use real estate, stocks, and bonds as the lure. Even 'reputable' multinational corporations, accounting firms, and banks are all capable of being nothing more than a large-scale con. While the short con can deprive a victim of few to a few thousand dollars, the big store cons are especially destructive capable of destroying an entire nation's economy.

The after effects of the these psychopaths are usually financial devastation along with all the repercussions of broken marriages, suicides, alcoholism, domestic violence, drug addiction, and ruined lives.

<u>Malevolent Psychopaths</u>:

More popularly known as Anti-Social Personality Disorder, or Sociopaths, the Malevolent Psychopath is the real life monster of our nightmares. These are the wife-beaters, murderers, serial killers, stalkers, rapists, sadists, pedophiles, gangsters, interrogators, and terrorists. They are usually career criminals and can amass an extensive criminal record while still in their early teens.[iii]

Often showing their contempt with a sneer or smirk and with a vacant stare from cold, predatory eyes, they are dangerous, unpredictable, and easily triggered into violence. Cowardly and sadistic they tend to target the most vulnerable in society, women, children, and the elderly and disabled. Often impulsive and opportunistic, sociopaths will not hesitate to commit any type of crime and will use manipulation, intimidation, and violence to get what they want.

The malevolent psychopath can show signs of their illness as early as age three. Early warning signs include compulsive lying, fighting, stealing, bullying, bad judgment, cheating, cruelty to animals, vandalism, truancy, sexual activity, fire-setting, substance abuse, and running away from home. The malevolent psychopath is the natural born killer.

<u>Professional Psychopaths</u>:

The malevolent psychopath is the most dangerous; however, it is the Professional Psychopath that is the most destructive. [iv] While the victims of the former can range

in the dozens, the victims of the professional psychopath can run into the tens of millions. These psychopaths litter history with genocides and the destruction of entire nations and empires. Historical examples include such monsters as Stalin, Pol Pot, Ivan the Terrible, and Caligula. While there are many that make it to the pinnacle of the political stage there are also such historical figures as J.P. Morgan, Randolph Hearst, and Mayer Rothschild, professional psychopaths that reach the pinnacle of the financial stage where they cause no less misery and destruction as their political counterparts.

The professional psychopath is just as malevolent, narcissistic, and remorseless, as the other stereotypes, they are just much smarter. [v] They can be found in any profession but usually governments, corporations, and religions will be thick with them.

In a corporation, the professional psychopaths are ideally suited for advancement. They can masterfully fake their abilities and credentials, us their intellect and charm to manipulate and exploit others, and generally backstab their way to high position. Once in power, their masks slip and they abuse their power and bully and sabotage their coworkers and subordinates.

In politics the professional psychopath's ruthlessness and cunning gives them a distinct advantage over any non-psychopath rival. They make charismatic leaders manipulating and brainwashing the naive, vulnerable, uneducated, or mentally weak. Mastery of lying allows them to make whatever outrageous campaign promises straight faced with, of course, no intention of keeping any of them. A life spent faking being human give them the ability to assume the roles of virtuous public servant, the perfect father, husband, advisor, mentor, and everyman. In addition when things get rough they have no inhibitions in playing dirty and readily resort to murder, assassination, persecution, war and genocide.

The third sphere of power that has traditionally attracted more than its fair share of psychopaths is religion. A quick glance at the history of religion from the bloody sacrifices of the Aztec priests, to the tortures of the Spanish Inquisitions, and through seemingly endless religious wars waged in the name of peace and love, makes their influence plainly visible to all willing to look. Since most if not all 'great' religions are constructed on falsehoods, compulsive liars make the perfect proselytizers. A look at recently created religions such as Mormonism and Scientology show their founders, Joseph Smith and L. Ron Hubbard respectively, were at least compulsive liars, and more likely full-blown psychopaths. Charismatic cult leaders such as Jim Jones and Sung Yung Moon were indeed psychopaths, while televangelist preachers that rake in millions from their gullible flocks are at best con artists of the highest caliber.

Religion's supposed *raison d'etre* of moral education and the veil of 'goodness' it bestows attracts psychopaths that use their membership in the religion as a cover, an extra sugar coating lest anyone suspect their true nature.

When psychopaths dominate and seize control of the major cultural institutions that influence a society a final type of psychopath is created.

Secondary Psychopaths: While the classic genetic psychopath is one who is born with whatever genetic trait that causes this pathology, there is another group of people that behave just like the classic psychopath who were not born that way but were created. Secondary psychopaths are created in two ways, through trauma and through groups.

Trauma from an accident, drug addiction, or severe physical and psychological abuse can destroy that part of the frontal cortex of the brain where empathy and conscience is processed. [vi] While such individuals are a tragic reality in our society, they are in most cases just as incurable as their genetic counterparts are. The exception is in drug induced Psychopathy. Most drug addicts will behave like psychopaths since the criminality of their addiction forces them to adopt Psychopathy as a psychological survival mechanism. With drug rehabilitation, they may regain their conscience, provided the drug use did not severely damage the brain itself.

The second way in which psychopaths are created is through groups. There are certain groups that will attract psychopaths because of the opportunities of power and influence membership provides. Usually such groups will quickly become led and dominated by psychopaths. Other non-psychopathic members of these groups would have to become psychopaths in order to survive.

For example, in a street gang, sociopaths make the best leaders and therefore most gangs have a sociopath at its head. Other psychopaths are also attracted to the violence and power of a street gang and so together they create a psychopathic value system. The gang becomes a psychopathic entity. The non-psychopathic youth who must live within the territory of such a gang is given two choices -become a victim of the gang or join them. By joining the gang, the new recruit must also adopt the group's twisted value system and behave accordingly thus becoming a secondary psychopath.

Conversely, at the other end of the scale we can see the same principle at work in corporations. The money and power of a corporation attracts the cerebral and narcissistic psychopaths. In a corporate environment they have many advantages over their non-psychopathic competitors for promotion. Not surprisingly most corporations end up being run by psychopaths. As with a criminal gang, a corporation's culture adopts the twisted values of its leaders. Those who would seek employment must likewise adopt or at least appear to adopt the corporation's essentially psychopathic mindset.

What is important to understand is that a mob has no conscience. Individual members may or may not have a conscience but when they are part of a mob, they will have none. Most organizations from street gangs to corporations are mobs. It would be a mistake to place your trust in them since they can turn predatory in a moment and deprive you of time, money, sanity and livelihood.

### The Psychopath's Modus Operandi

One weakness psychopaths have is that once one studies them and begins to understand them, they become predictable. While tactics vary from one to another, most psychopaths follow a similar strategy when conning either an individual or an organization. Their strategy is as follows.

<u>The Interview</u>: Psychopaths are experts at *Cold Reading*. First used by psychologists to describe what phony fortune tellers do 'Cold Reading', is the ability to guess a person's personality type quickly through verbal and non-verbal communication. The technique is simple, ask questions and watch the responses. Psychopaths will Cold Read you as part of what is called the interview stage. The whole purpose of the interview is for the psychopath to size you up as a potential victim. They make mental notes of different ways they could possibly manipulate you.

Learning to say less and observe more when first meeting people is the easiest way to defend against a psychopath. In social situations, you can be congenial without having to reveal personal information that could be used against you later. Remember that getting to know you is a privilege that should be earned over time.

<u>The Seduction</u>: Should you or your organization be seen as a suitable victim, the next stage is the seduction. Based on the results of their interview the psychopath will tailor the seduction to your personality. If concerned about your appearance, they will flatter your good looks, if insecure about your education, they will flatter you about your intelligence. If greedy, they will have insider information on a get rich quick scheme, and if cowardly then only the psychopath can protect you from your fears.

On a personal level, they will shower you with praise and attention in a whirlwind romance. They make sure that being around them is fun and exciting so that you become addicted to the adrenalin rush they create. On the organizational level, they pretend to be the perfect employee, the most devout follower, the most dedicated public servant. They work to ingratiate themselves first to the doorkeepers, and finally the power holders, often by being shameless sycophants and boot lickers.

At this stage of the game the best advice is the old canard 'If it sounds too good to be true – it is.'

Divide and Conquer: Just as a pride of lions will seek to separate a targeted *Wilde Beast* from the rest of the herd, so psychopaths seeks to isolate their victims from the rest of humanity. They accomplish this through the tactic of divide and conquer. In a personal relationship, the psychopath will sabotage and undermine his or her victim's relationships with family and friends.

Exasperated by the negative drama and costs associated with the victim, their friends and family drop out of contact leaving the victim without the support and guidance of their social group.

In an organizational setting, psychopaths are the consummate office politicians. They seek to create factions within the organization and then turn those factions against each other to create as much chaos as possible. Psychopaths swim in chaos and the more the better. Secretly they start to draw the gullible, weak minded, and fellow psychopaths to their side while intensifying their efforts to have the most talented, honest, and incorruptible members, ones that could have the strength of character to expose them, expelled. They poison the environment in a variety of ways so that everyone feels irritable, edgy, and unable to perform their jobs. Control of the organization slips into the hands of the source behind the dysfunction, the psychopath who created it all.

At this stage the only defense is to flee the situation. You cannot win this battle since the psychopath's ruthlessness will trump any counter attack you could conceive of. By the time you smell the smoke, the psychopath has already stolen the fire extinguishers. If in a relationship, cut bait and run. In an organization, find a new job, in a nation, become an expatriate.

Fear and Tyranny: The final stage of the psychopath's strategy is tyranny, the absolute and sadistic control over his victims.

In a relationship, the honeymoon is over and the mask comes off. The psychopath suddenly becomes controlling, abusive, and violent. Instead of flattery and attention, the tactics are now fear, intimidation, extortion, and emotional blackmail.

On the organizational level, ones see benefits being cut, while time cards, production quotas, and surveillance increases. Employees become slaves, powerless and disposable cogs in a machine run for the sole benefit of the psychopaths in charge.

On the national level, countries ruled by psychopaths become corrupt and brutish police states constantly at war with created and imaginary enemies. The population becomes paranoid, neurotic, and ultimately secondary psychopaths. In a psychopathic culture, everyone must adopt a ruthless attitude as a survival strategy.

At this stage there is little chance to flee and escape safely. Instead, you may be left with few options other than to tough it out and hope for rescue or for the psychopaths to die.

## Defense Against The Psychopath

<u>Facing Evil</u>: One of the greatest advantages psychopaths have is that average decent people cannot believe that such monsters truly exist. This inability to comprehend the predator mentality is partly due to popular morality. All societies promote simplistic and idealistic morality through schools and churches that teach such platitudes as, all men are created equal, everyone has some good in them, everyone is special, and so forth. Such ideals more often serve as a cover behind which the true machinations of society can operate without evoking the suspicion of the mob.

Another reason that people cannot face evil is fear. The true nature of psychopaths is the stuff of childhood nightmares. Many people simply cannot deal with the fear this realization causes and so to sooth their nerves they revert to an infantile strategy of denial and magical thinking. If they do not acknowledge the existence of monsters, then the monsters cannot hurt them.

The first line of defense against psychopaths is acknowledging their existence. By doing so, one develops a psychological advantage. Forewarned is forearmed and having braced oneself with knowledge of predatory individuals one is better able to think clearly and thus spot the predator before he can spot you.

Once you accept the reality that human predators populate our society the next line of defense is in identifying them. Because of their abilities at camouflage and deception, psychopaths are difficult to spot. They can fool even mental health professionals. It is important to understand that everyone can be conned. If you feel you are the exception, you only make yourself more susceptible.

Recognition: A psychopath is like a smoking ember. The sooner you can spot the smoke and douse the ember the better, since after the house is on fire it is too late to contain the damage and destruction. Learn to spot the typical psychopathic character traits, and recognize their modus operandi.

Where possible do background checks and/or speak with the suspected psychopath's family and friends. Most psychopaths leave a long trail of destruction and heartbreak and will try to cover their tracks. A lack of background information is therefore as suspicious as a history of betrayals. Another of their fundamental flaws is a lack of patience and the incredible energy they use to maintain their façade. Over time, they drop their masks. Thus, one of the best methods of detecting psychopaths is to wait them out.

Once you identify someone as being a psychopath you have only two options - attack or evade.

What Not To Do: What is vital to understand is that empathy cannot defeat the psychopath. You cannot change them, you cannot reform them, you cannot find the goodness inside them, you cannot show them the way to god, and you cannot teach them about love. All these approaches are doomed to failure since psychopaths can never understand nor can they care about these concepts. While they may lead you to believe that you are getting through to them, in reality, your empathy infuriates them and far from admiring your compassion, they despise you even more. While you try to 'understand' the psychopath, they are secretly calculating how best to cause you the most suffering. One must develop a cold exterior to them and view them from a distance. Do not pity them, feel sorry for them, or sympathize with them. [vii]

Attack: As a rule, the only thing that can defeat a psychopath is a bigger psychopath. However, should you feel no other recourse but to confront a psychopath your one advantage is their fear of being exposed for what they are. They have known since childhood that they are different from most people. Their whole advantage lies in the fact that they know what they are and no one else does. Exposing a psychopath takes away his or her advantage and reveals their inner corruption for all to see. However, few people have the strength and intelligence to do this successfully. While the statistical distribution of genius and idiot psychopaths mirrors the general population, even a moronic psychopath can elude and outwit an educated accuser.

Before you attempt to expose and expunge a psychopath you must be in a position of power, and you must choose the time and place. You also need to have your people briefed and ready to support you. This means creating a family and friends support group and/or joining a support group. In an organizational setting you need to have coworkers, managers, the legal department, and human resources on your side before making your move.

The Chinese strategist Sun Tzu warned against attacking an enemy who has no escape and likewise it is best not to corner a psychopath since the fight will likely be more vicious than most people can bear. Instead, use the threat of exposure to drive the psychopath away. The thought that they could be exposed at any time is unnerving and most psychopaths will give up the current game and go in search of more ignorant and vulnerable prey.

In an organization, you may have to offer not to press criminal charges if the psychopath will simply resign and never come back.

Evade: A safer and easier strategy is to evade. Once you have identified someone as a psychopath, you must cut him or her off and out of your life completely. In a relationship, you may need to change your locks, change you phone numbers and block your e-mail account, close bank accounts, get a restraining order, or move. Do not tip your hand that you are leaving. Be aware of the services of the police, law and shelters. Take self-defense and firearms training.

In conclusion, the study of Psychopathy is an important new tool not only in crime prevention, but in understanding the source behind many social ills. The more informed and aware you are of this subject the safer you and your family will be.

## Afterword to Defense Against the Psychopath

Disclaimer: The author is not a psychiatric or medical professional. This article is a brief overview of key points from other professional researchers, and intended to be used in the study of self-defense and crime prevention.

Since the video on Defense Against the Psychopath came out, there are three issues that have been raised and which I will try to address here.

The first issue is the argument that because everyone has good points and bad points, anyone could be viewed as a psychopath. The answer is that psychopath's motivations are qualitatively different from normal people. Many average people can behave badly for a variety of reasons such as poverty, ignorance, group pressure, substance addiction, emotional turmoil and a host of psychological ailments. For these people, if one removes the underlying circumstance that drives them to criminal activity, they would not behave that way. However, for the psychopath, criminality is the preferred choice regardless of their personal circumstance. Recent research suggests that the brains of psychopaths are fundamentally different from other people. Therefore, there is no grey area between psychopaths, and 'Normals'. Psychopaths are different.

The second question that often arises is, are psychopaths evil? The term 'evil' is a moral/religious term and thus problematic from a scientific viewpoint. Essentially, yes, psychopaths are evil, but this may not be their fault. We know that their brains function differently and that this may have a genetic cause.[1] A psychopath therefore could not have made the choice to be born a psychopath. Similarly, one cannot say that a tumor is 'evil' since it is likewise a genetic aberration. Absolving psychopaths of ultimate moral

---

[1] Dr. Kent Kiehl, *Psychiatry Research*, in 2006,

Adrian Raine, D.Phil, Biological Psychiatry (January 2004) and Archives of General Psychiatry (November 2003),

Professor Declan Murphy,Dr Michael Craig and Dr Marco Catani, 'Altered connections on the road to psychopathy', published in Molecular Psychiatry.

Robert D Hare, Craig S Neumann, "Psychopathy as a Clinical and Empirical Construct". *Annual Review of Clinical Psychology (2008)*

responsibly however, does not mean we should tolerate them in our affairs, for like a tumor, if allowed to continue, they will destroy everything around them until finally destroying themselves.

The third issue is the assumption that because we are labeling a certain segment of the population as undesirable, that this would naturally lead to persecutions and extermination camps. Any program of rooting out and neutralizing psychopaths would be doomed from the outset, since the psychopaths would quickly subvert such a program and turn it against the common people, as they have done throughout history. Furthermore, nothing so dramatic is needed since just by identifying the psychopaths in our society we undermine their strength and advantage. Then, in order to create a better society for all, we need do only three small things. Do not vote for them, do not worship in their churches, and do not buy their products.

S. Verstappen

# Recommended Reading

*The Mask of Sanity,* Hervey M., Cleckley ,Emily S. Cleckley; 5th edition
(November 1988)

**Without** *Conscience: The Disturbing World of the Psychopaths Among
Us*, Robert Hare, D. PhD, The Guilford Press; 1 edition (January 8, 1999)

*Snakes in Suits: When Psychopaths Go to Work*, Robert Hare, D. PhD,
Harper Paperbacks (May 8, 2007)

*People of the Lie: The Hope for Healing Human Evil,* M. Scott Peck,
Touchstone; 2nd edition (January 2, 1998)

*Political Ponerology: A Science on the Nature of Evil Adjusted for
Political Purposes* Andrzej Lobaczewski, Laura Knight-Jadczyk Red Pill
Press, Canada,1998

**Bad boys, bad men: Confronting antisocial personality disorder**, D. W.
Black, London: Oxford University Press, 1999

# End Notes

---

[i] There are several diagnostic definitions such as Psychopathic Personality Disorder, Pathological Narcissism, and Anti-social Personality Disorder, that describe a person that has no conscience.

[ii] "If I could have a choice of where to research psychopaths I would like to study those that work at the stock exchange." Robert Hare,

[iii] Sociopaths, who comprise only 3-4% of the male population and less than 1% of the female population (Strauss & Lahey 1984, Davison and Neale 1994, Robins, Tipp & Przybeck 1991), are thought to account for approximately 20% of the United States' prison population (Hare 1993) and between 33% and 80% of the population of chronic criminal offenders (Mednick, Kirkegaard-Sorensen, Hutchings, Knop, Rosenberg & Schulsinger 1977, Hare 1980, Harpending & Sobus 1987). Furthermore, whereas the "typical" U.S. burglar is estimated to have committed a median five crimes per year before being apprehended, chronic offenders- those most likely to be sociopaths- report committing upward of fifty crimes per annum and sometimes as many as two or three hundred (Blumstein & Cohen 1987). Collectively, these individuals are thought to account for over 50% of all crimes in the U.S. (Loeber 1982; Mednick, Gabrielli & Hutchings 1987, Hare 1993).

[iv] Dr. Hervey Cleckley discussed the "partial psychopath" when he talked about "incomplete manifestations or suggestions of the disorder" in psychiatrists, physicians, businessmen, etc. "Compensated" psychopaths were described as the subclinical psychopath or subcriminal psychopath by the famous Dr. Robert Hare.

[v] Hervey Cleckley (best known for co-authorship of The Three Faces of Eve), a pioneer in the field who provided the first coherent, thorough description of what he called the "psychopath" (and the "partial" psychopath), wrote: "Although they occasionally appear on casual inspection as successful members of the community, as able lawyers, executives, or physicians . . . . [t]he true difference between them and the psychopaths who continually go to jails or to psychiatric hospitals is that they keep up a far better and more consistent outward appearance of being normal."

---

vi Since the injury, J.S. fulfilled the DSM-IV criteria for Antisocial Personality Disorder (DSM-IV, 1994). J.S. `failed to conform to social norms' and was notably `irritable and aggressive'. His episodes of property damage and violence were frequent and were elicited after little provocation; e.g. an alteration in routine. He was `reckless regarding others' personal safety'; on one occasion he continued to push around a wheelchair-bound patient despite her screams of terror. His `lack of remorse' was striking; he never expressed any regrets about the nurses he hit. He failed to accept responsibility for his actions, justifying his violent episodes in terms of the failures of others (e.g. they were too slow). He frequently `failed to plan ahead', leaving the hospital regularly to wander about London with `no clear goal for the period of travel or clear idea about when the travel will terminate'. He showed `an inability to sustain consistent work behaviour'. Since the accident, he could not hold employment due to his interpersonal difficulties. In summary, J.S. fulfilled the criteria for acquired sociopathy except that he lacked premorbid aberrant behaviour. From: Impaired social response reversal A case of `acquired sociopathy' R. J. R. Blair and L. Cipolotti

**Brain**, Vol. 123, No. 6, 1122-1141, June 2000 Oxford University Press

vii Martha Stout, in her book *The Sociopath Next Door*, identifies what she calls the pity ploy. Psychopaths use pity to manipulate. They convince you to give them one more chance, and to not tell anyone about what they have done.

**The Art of Urban Survival,**

A Family Safety and Self Defense Manual

Language: English

Page Count: 304 pages

Size: 6.14" x 9.24" Perfect Bound Paperback

US$24.95

ISBN 978-0-9869515-0-3

This is an encyclopedia of crime prevention and disaster preparedness knowledge that covers a wide spectrum from; what to do if your child has been abducted, to how to decontaminate after being exposed to nuclear fallout. From; how to tell if someone is lying, to the three basic tactics used by predators.

Written in a 'just what you need to know' style with a no-nonsense understanding of what real life dangers entail, this material is easy to understand, follow, and suitable for the whole family.

www.chinastrategies.com

Defense Against the Psychopath is a brief study guide to teach people how to recognize and defend against our society's most dangerous, and often seductive, predators.


*The urge to save humanity is almost always a false-face for the urge to rule it.*
*H.L. Mencken*

Made in the USA
Lexington, KY
22 May 2014